This book is dedicated to Astronaut
Dr. Anna Fisher, Pele's Mummy
and the first mother in space!

Dr. Anna Fisher & Finse on board Viking Sun

THIS BOOK
BELONGS TO

"Finse Explores the Universe Planets"

The right of Karine Hagen to be identified as the author
and Suzy-Jane Tanner to be identified as the illustrator
of this work has been asserted by them in accordance
with the Copyright Designs and Patents Act 1988.

Text copyright © Karine Hagen 2018
Illustrations copyright © Suzy-Jane Tanner 2018

First published by Viking Cruises 2018
83 Wimbledon Park Side, London, SW19 5LP

ISBN 978-1-909968-23-3

www.finse.me

Produced by Colophon Digital Projects Ltd,
Old Isleworth, TW7 6RJ, United Kingdom
Printed in China.

FINSE EXPLORES THE UNIVERSE
UNIVERSE
PLANETS

Karine Hagen
Suzy-Jane Tanner

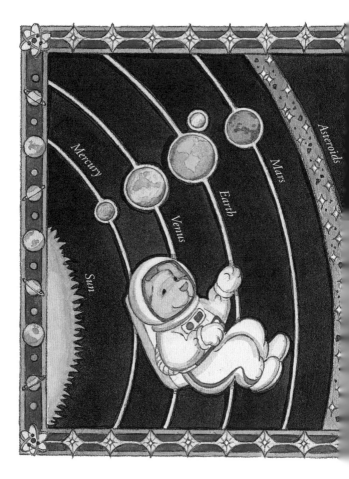

Mercury

Venus

Earth

Mars

Asteroids

Sun

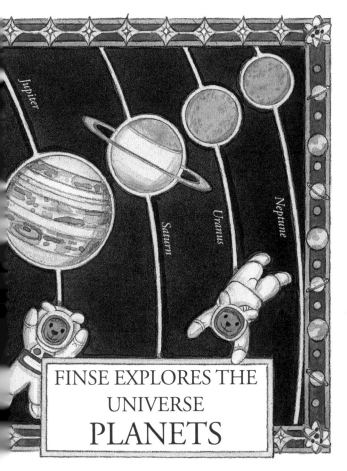

Jupiter

Saturn

Uranus

Neptune

FINSE EXPLORES THE
UNIVERSE
PLANETS

HIGHCLERE CASTLE

I have always been interested in astronomy and was very excited when my dogmanaut friend Pele visited Highclere Castle, my puppyhood home.

She told me about her work on the International Space Station. I was thrilled to hear I could join her and learn about exploring our Solar System.

TRAINING

But first I had to train at the Johnson Space Center in USA and Yuri Gagarin Dogmanaut Center in Russia. I learned mathematics and science, which are important subjects at school.

I practised in a special machine to learn how to cope with increased gravity during the journey and living in weightlessness on the International Space Station.

SOYUZ SPACECRAFT

When I had passed all my tests, we travelled on the Soyuz spacecraft. There was not much room on takeoff.

Once in orbit we could take off our spacesuits as we approached the International Space Station.

When we arrived, I felt sick for a little while. Then I was very hungry!

I enjoyed floating without gravity though my compass did not work in space. We could see the borders of the countries we came from but everyone felt like a citizen of the world.

We orbited Earth every 90 minutes and realised what a beautiful planet we come from and that we must take good care of it.

MERCURY & VENUS

Pele told me about space travel and our Solar System.

Mercury, the smallest planet, is named after the Roman messenger of the gods.

Venus, the hottest planet, is named after the Roman goddess of love. Several Venera missions have landed on the surface of Venus.

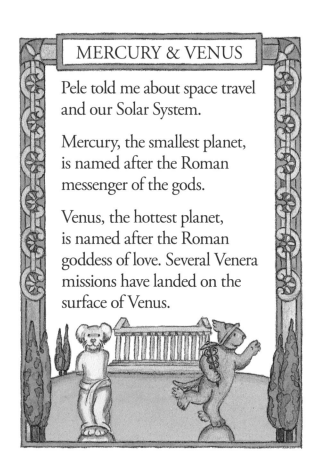

THE MOON

From Earth we see the changing phases of the Moon as it orbits our planet. Some farmers sow seeds at the waxing or waning phases of the Moon.

The first dogmanaut landed on the Moon in 1962. Because there is no wind there, his paw print will remain forever.

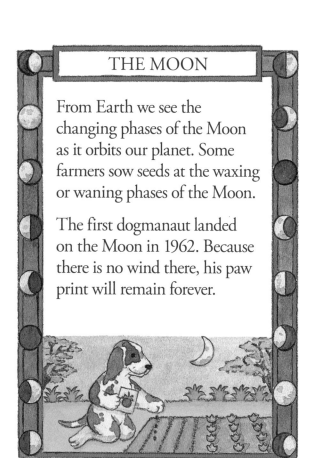

MARS

It was once thought little green dogs lived on Mars. The rover Curiosity has explored Mars and did not find any!

Pele, her mummy and friends at NASA have been working on the Orion Multi-Purpose Crew Vehicle, intended to carry dogmanauts to Mars and other destinations at or beyond low Earth orbit.

SLEEPING & EATING

Because of weightlessness on the International Space Station, we slept in special sleeping pods attached to the walls.

We ate from sealed containers of freeze dried space food and drank through straws as food and drink floats away.

It was fun trying to catch floating dog biscuits!

WASHING & HEALTH

Our bones deteriorate in weightlessness so we had to exercise. Without gravity, the ceiling can become the floor!

Because water drops float, we used wet wipes to wash. However much we brushed our fur, it still stood on end. There were special toilets so that pee and poo would not float away too!

JUPITER

The other dogmanauts told me about the outer planets.

Beyond Mars is the Asteroid Belt of small rocks and ice.

The further planets are huge gas giants. Jupiter is the largest planet in the Solar System. It is mostly swirling gases and liquids and has more than 60 moons!

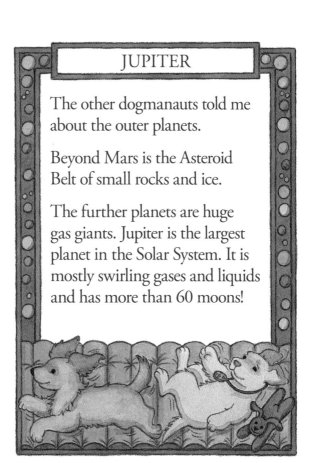

SATURN

Saturn also has many moons and the most spectacular ring system, which is made up of seven rings with divisions between them.

Since 2004, the Cassini spaceship has explored Jupiter then Saturn and its rings. It landed the Huygens probe on Saturn's largest moon, Titan.

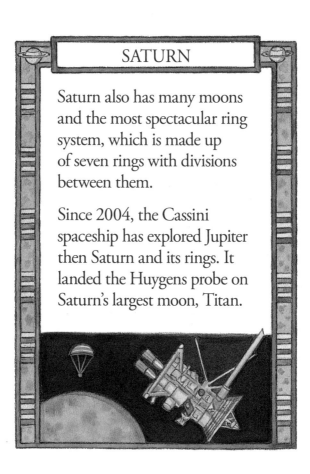

URANUS & NEPTUNE

Uranus rotates at a unique tilt, making it appear to spin on its side, orbiting the Sun like my favourite rolling tennis ball!

Neptune is a blue ice giant. The Voyager 2 spacecraft flew past Jupiter, Saturn, Uranus and Neptune. Now it is heading out of the Solar System.

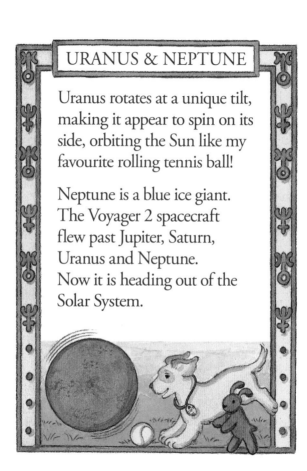

BACK ON EARTH

I returned to Earth on the Soyuz spacecraft. I had to be helped out as I felt very dizzy and five times my usual weight.

It was more comfortable to lie down but Pele explained we would recover more quickly if we walked. We enjoyed the fresh air and green plants in the garden.

I had been sad to say goodbye to Pele and my dogmanaut friends.

Now when I look at the night sky I can see the International Space Station passing overhead like a bright star. You can try to see it too, even without a telescope.

DOGOLOGY

As well as her Golden Retriever friend Pele,
Finse enjoyed meeting dogs from other nations
on her adventures.